Amaryllis Amaryllis

"How Does Your Garden Grow?"

"Organically of Course!"
By Marilyn Jansen

Amaryllis has a burning desire to share her love of gardening with others, and to inspire people to be planters wherever they live. In tiny apartments, in country homes, in neighborhoods or condominiums by the sea; anywhere on earth there's a place to plant. One of the greatest joys in life is to work in the earth and make things grow. Someone asked one day, "Amaryllis, Amaryllis how does your garden grow?" She replied, "with silver leaf trees, green and red ti leaves, yellow ginger, red ginger and plumeria trees all in a row. There are lovely white spider lilies surrounded by ferns. Caladiums and bromeliads love it in the shade of the monkeypod tree with spider plants, Japanese iris and wandering Jew.

Cymbidiums

My cymbidiums, oncidiums and phaleonopsis all grow in cinder and hapu fern like the Japanese ladies do.

The epiphytes with aerial roots grow so easily. They like the elevation up country I know. I learned that in a book about how certain orchids grow.

But mostly I've learned from others and by trying everything.

I keep them evenly moist but never overwater!

Dinnerplate Dahlia

My yellow dahlias are big as dinner plates! The purple tipped whites and the crimson reds are wild with color in a smaller version. The hot pinks with yellow centers are incredible!"

She found the need to plant became quite an obsession. Some people are born to plant and realize it one day like an awakening in their spirit that gives them so much happiness at the end of the day. This happened to Amaryllis with her first garden and became a lifetime of happiness!

Heavenly Blues

Her First Gardens

Her imagination would take her to faraway places where ancient gardens grew, outside castles in England or country farms around the world. She had no idea, when she began, about soil and water, or how to plan. She just got out there into the garden. Her soil was sandy, it had little nutrients; but she was more concerned with the design of her rows. She made the most unusual trenches that swirled in river-like forms and she imagined this is how a garden is planted. She placed the seeds carefully, as instructed on the package, one in each finger hole, about an inch apart, with a half-inch of dirt on top. For days she misted the squiggly rows until, seven days later, amidst the bare dirt, came little leaf pairs emerging from the earth. Each morning she'd look out to see how they were doing and sure enough, they grew into tall skinny zinnias. When they finally bloomed she had to laugh because even in the unhealthy soil they still presented many shades from salmon pink to magenta, bobbing on heavy heads almost falling over.

Amused, but not discouraged she decided to try Heavenly Blue morning glories. Their hard black seeds were shaped like tear drops.

She soaked them overnight to soften, then planted near the chain link fence to have a nice trellis for the vines to grow on.

Again in seven days or so the first two leaves emerged, and they looked like rabbit ears to her. The next leaf to appear was heart shaped and traveled in spiraling vines toward the fence top, along the links, twisting and turning wherever it wanted to, clinging tightly and vigorously until it reached the top where it began to tumble and reach outward into the air with nothing to grasp onto. Then, one morning, to her surprise, heavenly blue morning glories were all opened in glorious profusion, like magic flowers that were amazing.

She began to visit nurseries and opened her eyes to the neighborhood around her. She wanted to know everything that anyone grew.

She bought seeds and Organic Gardening magazine.

Mostly she used her sense of color and her imagination to make things beautiful. She learned about compost and mulching and adding to the soil.

She learned that it was most important to enrich, enrich, enrich.

Beside her fence there was a raised bed, formed by a short block-wall which she began to fill with dirt and sand and organic material to make a loose, rich, "loamy" soil.

She mixed in potting soils, about half regular dirt to half of the mix, until it felt nice to work with. She didn't know why, but she had to do this.

She planted California poppies amid carrots in a zigzag pattern, thinking how the lacy textures would be so delicate together. She planted in the fall and by spring the poppies had hundreds of bright orange blooms, which hid the carrots completely.

She planted comfrey and borage and herbs. She noticed the wonderful rich smell of the earth, and how time passed quickly when she was so absorbed in the beauty of making things grow. She experimented continuously with various plants. She learned about annuals (which grew only for that year) and that perennials were like grass; they grew and grew.

THE ROSE AND THE BUTTERFLY

She knew she wanted to be an Organic Gardener, because she could never use poisons or chemicals that could harm animals or human beings. Her Japanese neighbor lady also loved to plant. On her side of the fence were big sunflowers the size of platters, whose heads hung down when they were spent and birds came to enjoy the seeds.

Her neighbor also grew shiny black, long Japanese eggplants in her little plot, and in the front yard, she planted compact dwarf dahlias. One day, the lady gave her some seeds over the fence. She said they looked like a vegetable, the green was so vigorous. But Amaryllis discovered it was a flower, cosmos. The hot pink paper-like petals were a joy. They looked delicate but grew so thickly and waist high. They produced many seeds which she could replant, and thus began the joy of planting cosmos throughout her life of gardening.

California Poppies

Her first attempt to grow vegetables was quite a task. She tried the French Intensive method which required digging a one-foot-deep row, moving the top soil to the side, then digging the next row a foot deep, placing its soil into the first row, then row after row she repeated the process until the last row, whose trench was filled with the soil from her very first row. She had excellent results with beets and carrots, and turnips, but decided that in the future she would just dig deeply enough to prepare for planting and would always add compost to the earth.

Sweet Peas

This is how one discovers their favorites, sometimes by accident. Sometimes we must try and fail and start over again. A garden is for sharing. It develops character along the way, and as the gardener becomes more knowledgeable, it is shaped to his or her personality.

The most important thing is to try, and plant and plant and plant. Life is so rewarding when we dig inside ourselves to bring out the best to give to others.

The earth gives us so much beauty as God's gifts.
Try and discover every plant around you.
Find your favorites, or love them all, as you learn about flowers and plants.
It is not necessary to know the Latin names, but being a student of agriculture could enrich your life and the lives of many. You might learn how to produce a different species, or feed the starving populations, or create a healing cure for cancer.

The joys of gardening start within the heart.

There's something about watching things grow and how the leaves do shine that puts a smile on the gardener's face.

When they go to sleep at night their heart has such joy. The Hawaiians planted taro to prevent starvation. They planted with a passion, hundreds and hundreds of rows, because they had to. It was written by an old Hawaiian planter how he experienced such joy to look upon the huge leaves as they grew. As he laid his head down on the pillow, his spirit glowed inside.

He thought of the drops of water, how they looked on his large lush green leaves. He saw how they quivered in the breeze on their tall, sturdy stems, row upon row from the back of the valley down to the sea.

It gave such joy and satisfaction.

It is said the old Hawaiian planters were likened to the gardeners of today, because of their closeness to the land.

The planter remains the planter, not like the farmer who is "once removed" from the land.¹ A farmer uses machinery or animals to do the work.

Planters use their hands to create their wonderful works. Amaryllis knew she was like those planters for, deep inside her heart, she loved the earth with a passion and gardening was her fine art!

The imagination gets going!

The planters in Hana, Maui had to create their own soil, and built lava-walled raised beds for plant waste.

That was how they created their compost quickly.

Amaryllis always creates compost wherever she lives. Every scrap of vegetable goes into a lidded compost container she keeps nearby, on the counter of her sink, or just outside on the porch. Into it goes banana peels, papaya skins and seeds, potato peels, soybean skins, egg shells, coffee grounds; and even tea bags, napkins and paper towels; anything that can break down easily in the compost pile. Any type of vegetable matter is fine, and eggshells, which give calcium, are ok too. Nothing animal goes into the compost.

Daily she takes it down to the pile where she has dug a nice round hole in the ground about a foot deep. She layers the ingredients with grass cuttings, weeds, and various leaves.

It's important to add moisture to speed up the bacterial process, and to turn it to with the shovel or hoe aerate it, so that soon it will become the most beautiful soil. She loves to see the results of what otherwise would have been garbage. She never wastes a precious scrap that could contribute to the garden.

When a batch of soil is ready she fills up her wheelbarrow and moves it to the vegetable garden or flowerbeds or papaya trees and shovels on a nice layer of nutritious compost. The plants just love the rich nutrients. And the best thing we can do is add more.

Amaryllis finds it difficult to believe that so many lives are destroyed by drugs and alcohol.

If they wanted to know fulfillment they could find it by looking to God with all their heart and asking Him for a brand new life. With willingness to change and a truly repentant heart, He would show them the joys of gardening lead to a healthy and happy life!

It is the most wonderful joy to harvest a crop of fresh, healthy lettuce greens, and to pick baskets full of Roma tomatoes, green onions, fresh basil and thyme.

Amaryllis was so blessed with her first crop of Bibb lettuce, as well as her mesclun mix of arugula, romaine, tatsoi, bok choy, and other Chinese greens. She had started her garden in a small circle about six-feet in diameter.

The grass surrounded the circle where once a lemon tree grew. She had dug that out the year before.

She had turned the soil and dug it deeply, as always, and had turned over all the weeds to expose their roots to the sun and let them die. Any weed seeds were carried away. Then she watered the rich volcanic soil and continued to add compost daily, for a few weeks in preparation of her nice bed. Then she had loosened the soil again and pulled any new weeds by hand. She aerated with her small hoe and smoothed and leveled the dirt in preparation for the seeds and drew out her artistic pattern in the soil.

This time she drew a spiral, starting in the center, using a stick to create a small ravine. Into this she sprinkled her lettuce seeds being careful not to crowd them, then covered them with dirt and patted them down. Between the lettuce she planted borage, (an edible herb with blue flowers), and cosmos and calendulas.

She always mixes flowers with her vegetables to make her cottage gardens. In between, she plants green onions & mint to keep away pests. She had finished the circle by planting snap peas around the entire border. Then a two-foot chicken-wire ring was installed for them to climb on. She secured it to the ground with slim bamboo sticks. Tomato plants and basil were placed strategically in about six separate mounds. All this fit into the six-foot circle. When the lettuces were about two to three inches tall, she thinned them and transplanted some to other areas of the yard.

These became gourmet lettuces.
Her small patch produced over 100 heads.

She always plants basil among her tomatoes because she had learned long ago that basil, a companion plant to tomatoes, prevents the destructive tomato worm from coming around. The bushy, fragrant, green, sweet basil plant also compliments tomatoes in sauces and releases a unique scent. Just brushing by the basil plant takes one back to the first time they ever planted it, or experienced it for the first time.

Scent is like that. It evokes memory strongly. There must be a correlation between memory and scent and déjà vu.

On the Big Island of Hawaii ginger scent is in the air, along with molasses grass and guavas.

Hawaiian White Ginger

Just the mention of these scents makes Amaryllis yearn to go visit the Big Island of Hawaii. She envisions the puakinikini trees with amber or white colored flowers, and gardenias growing wild; they transplant so easily in Puna. Anthuriums are in her future. She hopes to grow pinks, reds, and whites in all sizes; and torch gingers and Hawaiian white ginger, too. She longs to collect orchids, as many as she possibly can. Varieties are unlimited on the "Orchid Isle", the Big Island of Hawaii. This joy of growing flowers and ferns and all things green is a passion for the earth and all living things.

The way life emerges is God's beautiful gift to us and provides our greatest joy!

It's a miracle the way that plant life springs from the cracks within the lava.

With enough moisture, ferns, wild orchids, huge Ohia trees, and coconut palms flourish amazingly. All the nutrients necessary for growth are apparently within the cinders.

She imagines in her mind the gardens she will have someday on the Big Island.

She can smell the ginger and molasses grass and see the raindrops beading up on the large green leaves of the taro root she will plant.

She can wander among the ancient growth of trees and ferns and orchids.

She loves to listen to the heavy rains when they come pouring down. The precious water will fill her 10,000-gallon tank and water all the ferns, palms, ginger and mosses. She envisions many greenhouses and growing plants for the rest of her life.

Ohia Lehua Trees

Hopefully others will be inspired to be organic planters of Hawaii. Paradise can be an example for the rest of the planet, of people working together in a small place to make monumental changes.

She has a vision for Hawaii !

With perfect weather for growing year round, it's a shame to let sunshine go to waste in such a magnificent land. In many places the soil has been damaged but it is possible to rebuild the soil. In three years, without toxins (chemical fertilizers or pesticides), and with constant amending with organic nutrients, one can rebuild the soil. So we must get to work enriching our earth and thereby our own lives.

Plant for the joy of it. Plant to eat.
Plant to save on groceries, plant because it's so easy. Plant for future generations some things you may never see mature.

Be like "<u>The man who planted trees</u>"[2] so unselfishly. He planted one hundred thousand and more, and changed an entire land in thirty years, because he felt sorry for the dry, dusty land.
His efforts inspired reforestations all over the world. He created an entire forest all by himself, just as he imagined.

So plant papayas trees and enjoy the fruit within a year or two, and plant citrus trees and coffee trees and lychee trees and mango and macadamia nut, and avocado.

Plant guava, and lilikoi and bananas. Plant mamaki and awa, and taro and coconuts and sweet potato.
Plant plumerias and ti leaf and puakinikini. Try valerian and echinacea and spearmint and peppermint; basil, sage, thyme and rosemary.

Oregano, tarragon, parsley and chives will thrive easily. Plant your lettuce, spinach, onions, string beans, carrots, turnips and daikon.

Start tomatoes and celery in flats, and then transfer them to the garden.

Try flowers of every kind, like hibiscus, bougainvillea, spider lilies and agapanthus.

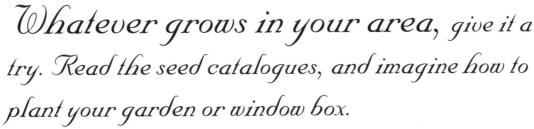

Try roses and dahlias, daylilies and cosmos; hollyhocks, hydrangeas, and morning glories; pansies, Johnny jump-ups, fox gloves, Siberian iris, zinnias, and poppies and pin-cushion flower.

Whatever grows in your area, give it a try. Read the seed catalogues, and imagine how to plant your garden or window box.

Maybe you have just a sunny window! In filtered light you can grow the most beautiful African violets, orchids, spider plants or ferns.

Plants need air and good drainage, so water them deeply on a weekly basis, draining them well.

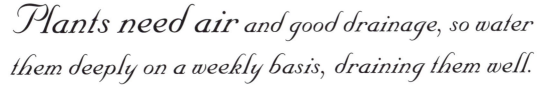

If a vegetable garden is your goal, then you must choose a sunny area that gets eight to ten hours of sun each day.

Your First Garden

Use your imagination. A garden is a work of art that will bring happiness for a long time. Start from where you are and take a look around. Ask yourself, "which areas do I want to make more beautiful?" It could be at the curb, by the mailbox. It might love alyssum and petunias, poppies and succulents. One might start with a circle around a big tree as the focal point of a first garden.

A path could be enhanced by a border of flowers or a bed of green onions. Imagine the fresh green edibles mixed with purple pansies or petunias. If there is only a small space, a potted garden or a window box can yield gorgeous results.

Remember that things that are alive give richness and beauty to any home. Do you see a farm in the future? Think big, but start small, so you can achieve satisfying results the first time.

Learn from others. Grandparents, aunties and uncles, friends, neighbors, nurserymen, books and magazines all have experiences to offer.

Amaryllis has planted so many gardens she cannot count them all, because she believes in planting wherever you live. Why wait to own? Life is so temporary, we must live now.

In Hawaii, she imagined a half-acre border with five-foot flowerbeds, all green and flowering in many varieties of plants and trees. And in one year she created it, just as she imagined!

Live now and plant it in the ground! Plants can be dug up, or cuttings taken, if you just can't part with the things you have planted when you must move on.

At a time when Amaryllis thought her life was ruined, gardening gave back to her the joy of life renewed.

My Garden Plan

Garden layout:

Kitchen Garden:

Herb Garden:

Cutting Bed:

Border Plants:

Trees to plant:

Compost Pile:

Seeds to Buy:

Plants to buy:

Bulbs to buy:

Organic fertilizers: organic fish emulsions, manure, blood meal, bone meal, limestone. (Organic Nitrogen, Phosphorus, Potash)

Pest control: Neem oil, neem cake, chickenwire

Preparation of the Soil
Compost

Start weeks, to a month ahead if you are just beginning to compost, for enriching the earth is the goal. Never waste a precious vegetable scrap, coffee grounds or eggshells. When you become an organic gardener, the joys of gardening will help the planet in many ways and it will reverberate.

Number One: <u>Beautiful, Rich. Soil</u>
Beautiful soil is created

Number Two: <u>Fewer Bugs Less Mess</u>
A clean place

Number Three: <u>Less Garbage</u>

When everything is recycled we create very little garbage and this saves the dump from filling up so fast.

Imagine everyone recycling!

The compost pile should be placed behind the trees or bushes where it won't be unsightly. Dig a hole about three-to five-feet in diameter and a foot deep.

Throw all the vegetable scraps and plant waste, (grass cuttings, leaves, old flowers, and cuttings) into the pile. Moisten it from time to time with a spray of water from the hose. Keep it moist, but not soggy.

Hoe or shovel once a week to turn it over and stir up the composting material to aerate it and speed up the process of breaking it down into soil.

A crated-type structure can keep the compost above the ground. Make it well ventilated with plenty of cracks between the slats. The early Hawaiians built up rock areas to contain their compost. There are commercially made compost containers. Layer the different ingredients like vegetable scraps, then leaves, then grass cuttings to avoid compacting the pile too tightly. In about four weeks, you will be amazed at the nice batch of rich, earthy soil that has been created. Start mixing it into the dirt where you plan to plant, or layer it around existing plants.

Garden Design

A garden reflects one's personality and how they like things to be.

Do you like a lot of color or just muted shades? What is your favorite color?

Would you prefer things very orderly and precise, or wild with color and shapes and everything imaginable untamed?
Is there a certain style you'd love, like completely Japanese, with raked gravel rocks and minimalism? Perhaps a shade garden is in your mind, and a sunny garden too. Dream a garden and make it happen. Just get started. The garden should be easy to tend so, in order to reach plants easily, keep beds about five-feet wide, maximum. Even better is a raised bed (a short walled area containing the soil) where one can sit on nice smooth bricks or stones and not have to bend over. Read the advice of the ancient gardeners and the gardeners of today.

It is so interesting to imagine the "Olden days".

Thomas Jefferson loved his gardens and designed those at Monticello.

Gertrude Jekyll is a famous garden designer of England.

The famed gardens at Giverny painted by Monet are an inspiration.

There's the Huntington Memorial Museum and Gardens in Pasadena, California, as well as Descanso Gardens.

In Hawaii, there are many botanical gardens to inspire the soul.

When Amaryllis began, it was simply because her father didn't want the dirt in the house. So she said "ok, I'll plant outside", and plant she did, for the rest of her life. She learned that landscape designers like to start with some formality or structure to give the garden form. This gives a focal point to draw the eyes to. It could be:

- A pond or waterfall
- A gazebo or bench
- A pathway of stone or brick or redwood chips, grass or gravel or sand.
- A row of trees that give magnificent form
- A layout of areas that take one on a journey throughout many gardens
- A beautiful gate that leads one in to a garden

You can start with just a patch of land anywhere that is pleasing.

A kitchen garden is best near the kitchen, so the chef can get herbs and vegetables easily.

Let's get started with the basic tools used in gardening.

Basic Tools

Before Amaryllis began gardening, she found the most amazing treasure one day. It must have been an omen because hidden inside years of overgrowth of vines and vegetation, outside the French doors at her apartment, she discovered an old hand-sized shovel suspended in the vines. It was made of a single piece of metal. It is strong! It has been her favorite tool for many years. She has cultivated and dug by hand many a garden with this trowel. It was three years after she found this trowel that she planted her first garden.

Keep it Simple

Garden gloves to prevent blisters and calluses.
Hand sized shovel
Hand sized claw (for cultivating)
Flat-blade shovel with short handle
Large and small hoes
Rounded blade shovel for carrying & digging
Grass rakes (narrow and wide)
Claw rake (for removing stones and for leveling)
O'o (heavy metal rod poker for deep holes)
Hula hoe (especially for flat weeds)
Pick axe (for hard dirt and ditches)
Sturdy shoes & rubber boots (for muddy areas)
Wheel barrel

Hand pruners for pruning & cutting flowers
Clippers for trimming branches & gingers

Did I forget anything? Amaryllis doesn't use much more.

Let's Get Digging!

It's the best exercise! It's great for the heart and increases aerobic activity. Proper picking, hoeing, and shoveling tightens the abdominal muscles. You must use your back properly and bend your knees. Rest is essential, so take a moment and drink plenty of water too. Make lemonade, or iced tea and enjoy the shade. Use sunscreen if you will be in the sun, wear a hat to protect your face and wear a shirt. It is best to work in the morning, or the late afternoon, to avoid the strongest ultraviolet cancer-causing rays. Besides, it's much more enjoyable when it's cool, and the light is so beautiful in early morning sunlight and late afternoon. Amaryllis suggests that for photography, the best light for beautiful natural color that is not washed out by bright sunlight is in early morning or late afternoon.

Soak an area for a few days by watering twice a day to soften the soil.

First create the framework.

Amaryllis draws with a stick in the dirt, whether it is a circle, a square, or a river-like border. Some like to place stakes in the corners, and tie string to the stakes to define an area.

Keep it simple and fun.

There is beauty in simplicity. Have you seen a flat of wheat grass? Imagine a beautiful border of chives or green onions.

Start digging.

The soil should be softened by the previous days of watering, or perhaps it is spring and the winter snows or rains have softened the ground. Amaryllis has worked in some of the roughest, rockiest conditions, and has succeeded in improving the soil, having plants thrive, by choosing plants that are hardy, drought-resistant, and mostly by adding composted organic material to soil from which most of the rocks have been removed.

Sometimes, there have been so many rocks she has just planted around them.

There is always a solution.

Amaryllis likes to use the flat bladed shovel to create a nice edge to define her garden. Then she hoes to loosen the top layer of soil. Clumps of weeds and grass roots are loosened and exposed to the sun. She throws all the debris to the side, for the compost pile, then hoes and hoes to break it up. She uses the round shovel to dig a foot deep.

It is important to rest, because this type of work can be very hard, but it feels sooooo good! Her hands get dirty, and the gloves, too. But she washes them often and pampers them later. She goes through a lot of tennis shoes in the dirt, but it's worth it. Some people prefer good work boots for the digging part and rubber clogs later for watering, and weeding and cultivating. She prefers tennies and then slippers (thongs) for later.

So loosen all your soil a foot deep, in three-foot sections, then dig it, chop it, and remove all the weeds rocks and debris to the side.

The green waste goes into the compost, and the rocks go wherever you can use them for borders, or for drainage; or stash them, or haul them away.

Amaryllis always does this part by hand. She has never used a roto-tiller, because she was afraid of the rocks flying. She loves to dig anyway. That's how she stays in shape.

When the soil seems to be all loosened deeply, rake it smooth and spray with water to keep the dust down and to moisten.

Planting your garden

Have you dreamed your garden? There is nothing like the healing of the soul and spirit which gardening gives to the planter. For those who need instant gratification, that is possible, too.

Structure

When Amaryllis designs a garden, or flowerbed, or border, she always starts with some feature that will give instant beauty.

It might be the rock border of blue lava rock itself. A row of ti-leaf plants to line the drive can give instant formality and beauty.

Did you know the ti-leaf was brought here by the Hawaiians from Polynesia? It is planted by putting it into the ground and watering it well. The stalks can be cut into short lengths to start, but Amaryllis likes to get a head start on their height, so she starts her ti-leaf plants at least 2-3 feet tall. They survive beautifully if watered consistently for the first few weeks. Some leaves will yellow and fall off, but soon they will recover and thrive.

A line of Manila palms is stately and elegant and so beautifully shaped.

Plumeria trees give scent and instant beauty and are planted easily from cuttings. Start with branches about three-feet-tall to get a head start on your plumeria trees. Plant them on the windward side of the house so the scent someday will blow through the home. It is best to break off pieces and let them harden off for a few days to seal the skin of the plant to prevent disease from entering. Then just stick them in the ground and water each day until they take root. Once established, they can go days, or even weeks, without watering.

Succulents are treated the same way. They are her favorite drought-resistant plants.

Drip systems and sprinkler systems, on timers set to the cooler times of day when water is used most efficiently, are awesome.

Color

Succulents give instant beauty and color.

Clusters of succulents give instant design! Amaryllis loves blue succulents, and grays to contrast colors. Gray is excellent as a backdrop for color. Consider Dusty Millers to mix with ruby red snapdragons, cobalt blue lobelia borders, bright green carpets of small ice plants, and even red rhubarb or chard as colorful blend. Purple kale, is a gorgeous ornamental plant to be used for color, even if you don't eat it. Hawaii is a dream place for the planter. Nearly everything seems to grow.

Annuals

Amaryllis loves to start with whole flats of color, like pink or purple petunias, foxgloves, poppies, snapdragons, or pink lantana. For best effect she plants one color, or a variation of two colors! Cool colors come alive in low light!

Certain flowers, like zinnias, she plants from seeds, because they always do better. They seem to harden off better in the ground, rather than getting shocked by the transplant. Annuals are replaced annually, and even more often if you like. They are inexpensive and great to experiment with color. For instant effect and curbside appeal, try annuals in bloom already!

Perennials

Perennials continue to grow year after year. They can be divided at the roots. Lavenders in four-inch pots will mature in three years. They are drought resistant, have scent and beautiful color.

Rosemary is a hardy perennial with woody stems. Certain oriental poppies are perennial. They reseed also. When the flowers are spent, they get cut back and come again every spring. Flax and yarrow are the same. Perennials give structure and formality to the flowerbeds. Choose carefully. When they are not in bloom, select annuals for color!

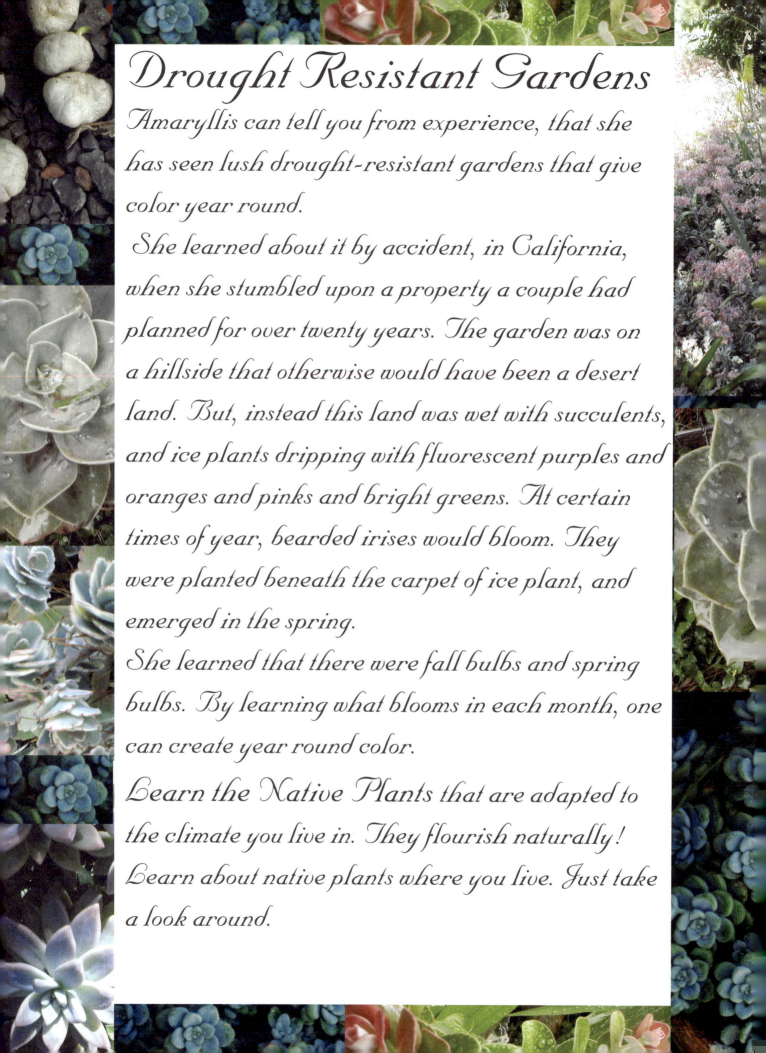

Drought Resistant Gardens

Amaryllis can tell you from experience, that she has seen lush drought-resistant gardens that give color year round.

She learned about it by accident, in California, when she stumbled upon a property a couple had planned for over twenty years. The garden was on a hillside that otherwise would have been a desert land. But, instead this land was wet with succulents, and ice plants dripping with fluorescent purples and oranges and pinks and bright greens. At certain times of year, bearded irises would bloom. They were planted beneath the carpet of ice plant, and emerged in the spring.

She learned that there were fall bulbs and spring bulbs. By learning what blooms in each month, one can create year round color.

Learn the Native Plants that are adapted to the climate you live in. They flourish naturally! Learn about native plants where you live. Just take a look around.

Planting from Cuttings

She started her ginger from cuttings in Hana, Maui. Heliconias can be started from a root section and also spread with very little effort. Taro can be planted in dry land as well as wetland, and can be grown for beauty as well to be eaten. Amaryllis loves the huge leaves of the taro plant, and there are many varieties. She loves to eat poi, and lau lau (fish, pork or chicken wrapped in a taro leaf, tied in a ti-leaf package, and steamed to cook).

It is so delicious.

So many plants can be started from cuttings or divisions from mother plants and in fact, taro is symbolic of the Family, because it lives on and on. The mother root puts out keikis (children), which branch out and create new families of their own. When the root is dug up to be boiled and pounded into poi, the smaller roots are broken away from the mother root and replanted to make new crops. Ask your aunties or friends or neighbors for cuttings, or plants that need to be divided.

Get to know other gardeners who love to plant.

Other gardeners will share their knowledge and enthusiasm and always love to share plants.

Keiki (baby) banana trees are started from the new shoots that start from the mother plant. Cannas are divided in the same way. Beautiful reds and pinks with lush broad leaves are cut down after the blooms are finished, and the new shoots produce more and more blooms. They also spread easily, and require very little water.

It is amazing! They grow so tall. They can be contained to control growth, also.

Amaryllis started all her Hawaii borders from cuttings taken from various places. Her huge beds of cannas started from one package, purchased at the nursery. She has now divided and planted into several places. She buys her dahlia tubers at the local nurseries, but they can be purchased from catalogs by mail order, or online garden suppliers.

She had the most privileged experience of living on an estate for four years. It had been landscaped back in the sixties, by another lady who loved botanicals. She even discovered her old garden plan tucked inside a very old book called

"Exotica", a pictorial encyclopedia of indoor plants. On a faded piece of parchment paper, all the plants were listed in Latin as well as by their common names. Some plants had perished, but most were thriving well after more than forty years on Maui. This place captured a touch of old Hawaii.

The house was built in the forties, then moved, in the early sixties, to a higher elevation to avoid the tsunamis. Manila palms surrounded the courtyard wall. The palms had been moved from Kahului, also. They are so elegantly shaped and tall after forty years growth. Huge white spider lily plants were clustered beneath the palms surrounding the courtyard at the top of the drive. At the big iron-gated entrance to the drive, huge Dracaena dracos greeted guests dramatically.

    Often she would look out to see ladies picking up the leaves that had fallen, which they would weave into baskets. They had been collecting these for years, with the permission of the lady who owned the estate.

The outside garden of five acres was carefully planned and it is so exciting to imagine another lady planter. In the distance there was a very old grove of eucalyptus. The lady planned it so beautifully, on such a large scale.

With the eucalyptus grove as a backdrop, she planted Lau Hala trees, giving a prehistoric look, and complimented them with Dracaena marginata. She had an education in botany and a joy of agriculture. There was an autograph tree, (where names of lovers could be scribed in the leaves), a Japanese white flowering tree, and then a long long row of panax, about two hundred feet long, which screened the background of the property, where sheds and lumber and chicken coops at one time were hidden from view. It was so lush and refined looking. Though Amaryllis is self-taught, what matters most is that the same happiness comes to every planter.

Amaryllis imagined her garden as a mini-estate and planted small ti-leaf (Cordyline minima ehu-kai) to border the property. At the base of the ti plants, she planted "Pilea serpillacea."

In the shade of the monkeypod, she placed all her tall plants, near the back corner of her yard.

Yellow Hawaiian ginger and kahili ginger does beautifully among the spider lilies, red and green coleus, and agapanthus in the filtered light.

To contrast all the green, she planted red caladium, for their unusual leaves, and variegated bromeliads added texture and shape.

Coffee trees enjoy the canopy of shade among the spider plants and lilies, and ferns of several types.

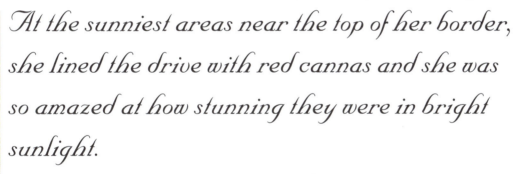

At the sunniest areas near the top of her border, she lined the drive with red cannas and she was so amazed at how stunning they were in bright sunlight.

Lau wae' ferns love the sun. (They don't seem to burn at all.) They spread along a root vine that travels underground.

Bright green finger-like fern fronds reach outward and straight up in their patch.

She has seen huge patches planted in Wailea, and Kahului.

Certain more delicate plants belong in the shade, like ferns, impatiens, and hostas. Spider plants thrive in the shade or at the north side of the house. Their color is vibrant green and white striped, and they look so fresh and alive in the shade. In the sun they appear all washed out and faded. So learn what loves shade and which love sun. The sticks in the potted plants you buy at the nursery will tell you.

They do well in a tight pot with good drainage, and they let you know when to replant to a larger pot. (They will burst the pot when the roots are too big). In the ground, they put out runners from the babies, and make a nice patch of spider plants.

Amaryllis loves so many plants, it is hard for her to choose, so she plants whatever she can, wherever possible, using common sense.

Amaryllis continued to plant the half-acre border and completed the planting in one year. It was done in three sections, each taking really no more than a few weeks of adding plants. She spent very little money on this planting as most were started from cuttings.

However, she did buy her Mandevilla vines, stephanotis vines, pikake plants, coffee trees, and dahlias, as well as her annuals. The basic green lush landscape was created for free, with just her labor of love.

The Mandevilla vine is watered by the washing machine and it spills over the fence to the neighbor's yard where everyone can see a cascade of big white flowers, growing wild.

In phase two, along the long fence at the bottom of her yard, she kept starting coleus in reds and greens. The coleus grew to waist high. Plumeria trees took two years to establish themselves. Papaya trees grew quickly.

Spider lilies became huge in three years and bloomed for the first time. These were all started from the bulbs that fall over from the flowers, once they are all spent. They fall to the ground, and hundreds of new spider lilies start growing. She collected hundreds of these to start her mini-estate. She clustered them together to create immediate effect. The bright green blades create instant beauty.

When they get too thick, she divides them for other places. Among the greens, she dug into the earth and planted dahlia tubers. She puts bone meal in the hole to boost the growth, and nourish the bulb, and stirs it up in the dirt, then places the root in the hole and covers with soil. In a few weeks, healthy green leaves appear, and soon grow tall and produce amazing flowers in so many varieties.

Though unscented, dahlias are unique & flamboyant. They add character and wildness to any bouquet. She likes to mix her dahlias with gardenias, zinnias, cosmos, heliconias and herbs like basil, and ferns and anise or fennel into huge bouquets to give away. People are so surprised, because they are not common in Hawaii.

Plant What You Love

Amaryllis once met a Japanese girl in New York City. She had been raised on the island of Maui, Hawaii, had moved to the middle of Manhattan, and lived in a brownstone building. To make it feel like home she had saved the top of a pineapple and planted it in a large terracotta pot.

The pineapple is actually in the bromeliad family. Amaryllis plants every pineapple top in the garden throughout her borders, more as a dramatic effect. She loves their beautiful blades as they take hold in the earth, and shoot upward and outward in star-like multiple layers of gray-green spikes that curve outward. Intense!

First she places them in a glass of water to develop roots and then plants the pineapple tops in the ground. Water them well and they will take root!

Dream in Color

    Often Amaryllis dreams in color.

    She saw flats of purple-violet lavender plants surrounding her friend's house and hillside. The upper decks spilled vibrant purples reaching toward the sun. Behind the house, out the kitchen window, flats of solid purple color burst up toward the sky above the brick wall.

    Wind chimes echoed in the breeze.

    Beautiful sounds, beautiful color, healing the spirit.

    Different plantings came to her via the subconscious mind. She remembers a dream of long beds of pink and white carnations. Skinny grayish blades in round clusters as if they'd been established for years, looked like an old garden.

    In another dream she saw old bearded irises in champagne color and purples that were clearly planted years ago in raised beds at the back of a large yard.

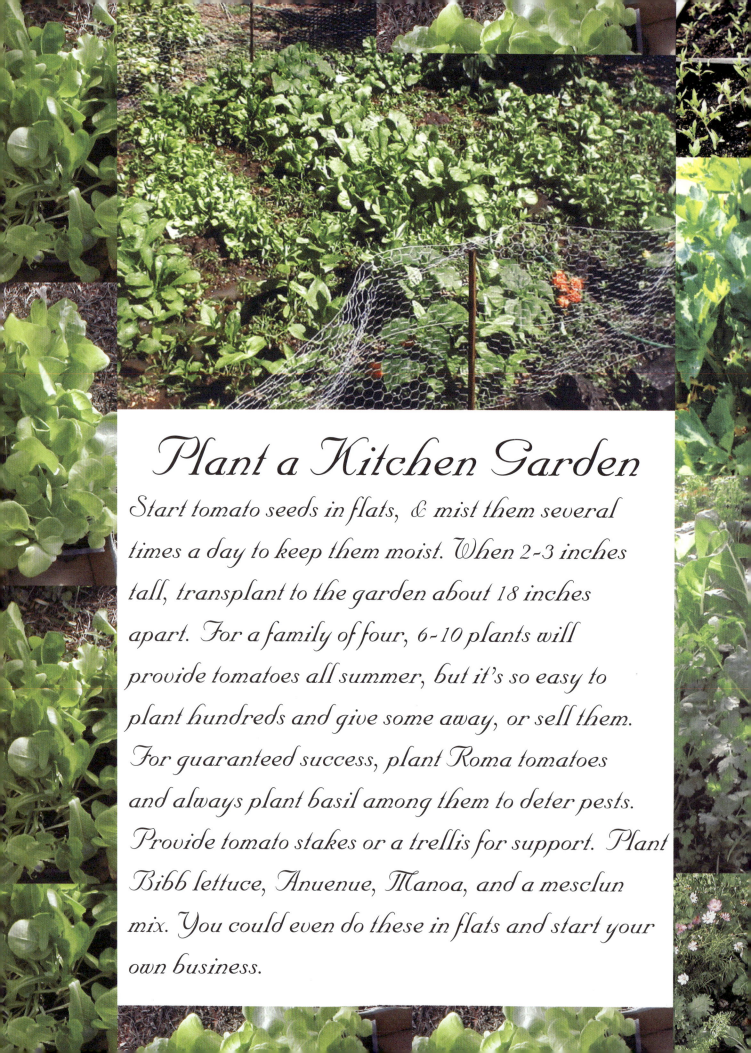

Plant a Kitchen Garden

Start tomato seeds in flats, & mist them several times a day to keep them moist. When 2-3 inches tall, transplant to the garden about 18 inches apart. For a family of four, 6-10 plants will provide tomatoes all summer, but it's so easy to plant hundreds and give some away, or sell them. For guaranteed success, plant Roma tomatoes and always plant basil among them to deter pests. Provide tomato stakes or a trellis for support. Plant Bibb lettuce, Anuenue, Manoa, and a mesclun mix. You could even do these in flats and start your own business.

Imagine beautiful geometric raised beds planted in a variety of lettuces, purple, bronze, and green. Plant green onions, leeks, yellow onions, shallots and Bermuda onions. Plant turnips and carrots in a nice loose bed. Plant snow peas & snap peas and plant every two weeks to extend the crop. Plant string beans and make a tee-pee for them to grow on.

Plant zucchini & yellow crookneck and acorn squash, and Kabocha pumpkins where you have a lot of room. Plant squash seeds a few to a mound. The best one or two are allowed to grow and get big with squash. Don't forget eggplants, peppers and celery too. *Plant herbs of all kinds.* (Parsley, sage, rosemary, thyme, sweet basil, Thai basil, lemon balm, chives, tarragon, & lemongrass.) Try cilantro, oregano, borage and sorrel. Follow the instructions on all the seed packets. Follow your dreams of a beautiful garden. Be creative!

A Cottage Garden

A cottage garden is an Amaryllis favorite. It's how she dreamt a garden should be (Frilly and old-fashioned, from another age). She saw muted purples and pinks and white fox-gloves. She saw a garden of

Tall blue delphiniums in the back, dark colored single hollyhocks, and climbing roses over the cutting bed of zinnias. Russian sage attracted butterflies, complimenting purple and blue salvias. There were deep purple campanulas, and coral-bells, violets and primrose.

Oriental poppies reseed themselves. Penstemmon and foxgloves and snapdragons are a show of color in spikes, with clusters of flowers. She loves phlox and sweet peas along a country fence.

Cosmos gives it a lacy touch, with white yarrow for a drought resistant look of lace.

White alyssum gives an old fashioned look, and California poppies combine beautifully.

Roses

Amaryllis is not an expert on roses, but she has done quite a few plantings, inspired by a friend's mom who had dozens of rosebushes, including Sterling roses, the heavily scented lilac colored kind.

She learned that roses are not delicate just because they are luscious and beautiful. Thorns protect them from predators.

Roses continue year after year.
They can be started from cuttings!
She learned about tea roses, which grow one to a single stem, and climbing roses, floribundas (many clustered on a stem), cabbage roses and old roses.
Antique varieties were coming back.
She also learned about bare-root roses arriving in a burlap bag ready to plant after soaking their roots to bring them back to life.

In the mountains of California she had planted an oval bed of a dozen new rose bushes in many colors. (There were deep reds, whites, hot oranges, pinks and yellows.) An unexpected snow came a month later, and covered all her roses. They survived. A good start is all they need and irrigation wells, and a feeding now and then while buds are forming. When cold comes, they can be mulched to protect from freezing.

Companion plant to prevent pests.

How to Plant Roses

Dig a hole twice as big as the root ball. Break up the roots slightly and place around a mound of peat moss, mixed with soil, or rich loamy compost.

Fill the hole with soil and compost up to the base of the plant. Make a ridge around the circle, to make a well to hold water.

Avoid watering too late in the day.

Always prune back to the 5-leaf. The next rose will grow there. When pruning, they say to cut back to three main canes.

Roses love the mountains.

Old estate gardens with long rows are magnificent surrounded by long pathways of green grass.

Topiary roses are a lovely entry to a home. She loves a beautiful arch with climbing roses on an old fashioned lattice or a modern iron version.

Remember to feed them during blooming season with a dressing of bone meal, blood meal, or well-rotted manure, or a manure tea (made with manure in a burlap sack tea bag soaked in a drum of water). Pour this around the plants.

Pests

Certain pests might come along, so Amaryllis always does companion planting with marigolds nearby to deter aphids. Onions are planted in between, and mints and other herbs like thyme and rosemary, which are beautiful and help to keep away pests. If something attacks leaves, leaving a lacy patterned leaf, she prunes them back and starts over. She learned that pyrethrum was an ingredient in chrysanthemums, which repelled aphids, and could be used against nematodes organically. She learned that **neem oil** extracted from the seeds of the neem tree in India was safe and effective against aphids, white flies, bean beetles, corn ear worms, leaf bugs, squash bugs, cabbage worms, tomato worms, vine borers, thrips, and a multitude of pests, including sooty mold on her gardenia leaves and kaffir lime trees. She mixes it with a small amount of water in her pump sprayer and a few drops of castille soap to emulsify the oily substance so it mixes in the water. Then she fills up the sprayer with water and sprays the organic mixture as needed. (available at www.whiteflowerfarm.com, groworganic.com).

It has been suggested to spray garlic crushed in water, or chili pepper water, or tobacco crushed up in water, insecticidal soaps, or bugs crushed up in water. She hasn't tried them. Diluted dish detergent in a spray bottle is excellent for getting rid of the crab spiders that spin their webs in all the trees sometimes. For slugs she places trays of beer in the garden, beneath plants. Slugs and snails are attracted to the yeast and crawl in to drown. Remember to plant plenty for everyone, including a few pests, and best of all be a vigilant gardener. As you are watering, weeding, cultivating, and mulching, look under the leaves. Observe for worms, slugs, or evidence of damage. Healthy plants are less susceptible to disease.

You will find a solution.

She grabs any snails and bags them. She crushes worms on the spot. Most of the plants thrive, untouched by invaders. For larger creatures like bunnies, rats, deer and dogs, she uses barrier methods like chicken wire, and plastic mesh fencing, but also she plants things that they don't like such as foxgloves and peppermint, catmint, spearmint and the onion family. For gophers she has read that bulbs can be planted inside a container made of chicken wire. It's not hard to grow amazing gardens. It just takes a little imagination and desire, and a passion to beautify.

About Bulbs

Amaryllis learned all about bulbs at a nursery called Sassafrass. The owner was an English gardener named Pamela.

She learned that bulbs were seasonal! Fall bulbs were planted in the fall, for spring bloom and spring bulbs are planted in the spring, for summer bloom. There are early and late bloomers!

When doing a clients flower bed, the landscape designer would plant the one-gallon plants, like lavender and rosemary, roses and other small perennial shrubs. In between they planted the bulbs to come up later in the next season. They planted irises, tulips, ranunculas, daffodils, narcissus, lilies, alliums, hyacinths and snowdrops. Crocuses are short little plants. Siberian irises are miniatures. There are so many bulbs to plant each at their specific depth. One can learn from the packages how deeply to go. She has used a bulbing tool!

No matter what type, it's basically the same, you dig the hole deep enough and in the bottom of the hole put bone meal and blood meal mixed in the soil, and maybe some organic fertilizer to give them a little boost.

Cover them with the earth, and water them well, and then wait for their little points, or blades to emerge. Tulips like a good freeze, so if necessary, you may place in the freezer for two weeks before planting, and certain spring bulbs cannot take the cold. (Dahlias cannot handle a freeze).

So dig them up and store in a dark place in a bag until spring again. In Hawaii, she leaves them in the ground. In spring, she clears away areas that have overgrown, so her dahlias will be able to see the sun, and nurtures them with a dose of plant food like bone meal, or organic fish emulsion. She learned about "forcing" bulbs by planting them indoors, on a bed of smooth rocks, above water, set in a shallow tray. Narcissus bulbs were forced to bloom within weeks, without an inch of soil. Soon roots reach down to the water and green blades came straight up, blossoming soon after.

Bulbs are so interesting. They live dormant beneath the soil, and emerge when the weather is good and all the conditions just right.

For spring she plants her favorites (dahlias, dahlias, dahlias). In California she plants freesias. Bulbs also do well in pots, clustered tightly. She mixes Dutch irises, daffodils, tulips, ixias, ranunculas, and anemones in a wide terracotta bowl. She leaves the gladiolus for others, and prefers miniature Siberian iris, and fuscia colored ixias with a stem as thin as a wire. Black tulips are dramatic arranged in a fishbowl with clear glass stones at the base to hold them in place.

Bulbs can be ordered from catalogs or purchased in nurseries. It's exciting to imagine your bulb garden coming up at different times. There are stories written about bulbs like "The Secret Garden". Snowdrops will naturalize (spread on their own). Irises and many others can be divided when they get overgrown.

Daffodils will multiply year after year. She loved how they popped up through the snow in early spring, in the mountains of California. She learned there was a difference between bulbs, corms, tubers, and rhizomes. Most bulbs are bulbous in shape. Tubers, have tubular roots branching out from the main root. Rhizomes, such as bearded iris, and gingers, have a tough skinned root, which can be cut to into other pieces to be replanted. They do much better when divided out of their crowded beds. Ranunculas have their own rooty shape pointed toward the bottom of the hole. Anemones are hard little odd shaped things. Look for the top to place them properly. Have fun, and imagine the results. They will be amazing!

Nai'o

Native Hawaiian Plants

Amaryllis wanted to learn all about Hawaiian plants. In one day, she learned about 16 native species by visiting the Native Plant Nursery at Ho'olawa Farms in Haiku, Maui. They've planted over 120 varieties. They are the largest grower of Native plants in the state of Hawaii. Anna Palomino took her all around the nursery, explaining the types of plants, what they were used for, their preferred climates, whether they were endangered, and where they were found. She learned about 'Ae'Ae (Bacopa monnieri), a glossy, dense, flat-growing lush green carpet. She learned panohiiaka, "skirt of pele's sister", is a beautiful groundcovering. She learned that "uki uki" was a native lily, and prostrate naupaka (endangered) was grown from cuttings or seeds. It was similar but different than the more common beach naupaka.

She loved pohinahina, a coastal purple flowering plant that grew strong circular shaped leaves so geometric, yet soft looking.

The Lo'ulu palm (native fan palm) is native to East Maui. Nai'o is false sandalwood. Alahee is a large shrub with glossy green leaves.

The endangered Marselle, found on Kauai, is a delicate looking plant that looks like four-leaf clovers. Aki aki is a native grass found in sand. Ili-ahi is coastal sandalwood. Olu olu, also called "cabbage on a baseball bat" is found only on Kauai and Niihau. The National Botanical Gardens on Kauai has a seed bank.

Uki Uki

Mao'

The Mao' is a cotton plant. It has been bred with commercial cotton to produce disease resistant strains.

Ohai

Ohai, a small tree with its orange flowers reminded her of Molokai, which still looks wild and native.

Ilima Papa

Ilima Papa is an orange flowered flat ground cover easily maintained and excellent for hillsides.

Pohinahina

Now when she walks along the path in Wailea, she recognizes all the native plants and feels what Hawaii looked like many years ago. Learning about these plants has made her feel more in touch with the land. She will start a native effort of her own, encouraging others to plant natives wherever they live.

Amaryllis called the Water Company to get the list of drought resistant Native Plants. They also informed her of the invasive species, like miconia (a large velvet leafed plant that can crowd or totally shade out native plants with its huge leaves), that must be eradicated.

It surprised her that yellow ginger shouldn't be allowed to spread into the gulches, because it can choke out areas also. Even loquat is mentioned in the "Do Not Plant" section, because it spreads so easily from seed pods that fall to the ground.

In order to recognize plants by their names, one must visit the botanical gardens and nurseries to identify and remember the names. Write them down, and something you liked about it. Try to take a quick sketch, or photo. This will help keep them in your memory and become a part of you.

The most important tip for planting natives is well drained soil. They will not tolerate soggy land. Mulch to control weeds.

Each native has specific areas in which they grow best.

1. Wet and windward areas.
2. Cool dry upper elevations.
3. Warm to hot low elevations.
4. Wetter low areas near mountains.
5. Windward coastal salt spray zones.

Places to view Native Plants on Maui are:

Ho'olawa Farms	Haiku, Maui	575-5099
Kula Botanical Gardens		878-1715
Maui Nui Botanical Gardens		249-2798
Kula Forest Reserve		984-8100
Kahanu Gardens	Hana, Maui	248-8912
Kahului Library Courtyard		873-3097
Wailea Point		

Call for appointment and directions first.

"Olu olu"

Native Endangered Species

While Watering

While watering, you can learn the art of relaxation. While sprinkling, or spraying your plants, and giving your trees their weekly soak, feel the moisture, and hear the water and enjoy the quiet moments to observe. One gets a chance to let their mind wander and relax and hear the birds singing in the trees. See all the different birds about, or maybe a chartreuse green Jackson chameleon slowly climbing a vine. While watering, the mind is calmed. Whenever there has been a stressful time, Amaryllis gets out into the garden and starts watering and feeling all the different environments she has created in her own yard. She feels joy and happiness and thankfulness among all her plants. She thanks God for blessing her so greatly and thinks that everyone should feel this way. While weeding or watering, she would stop and look out and see the pepper trees softly moving in the light breeze, and feel the coolness on her face, and see the shadows cast across her whole yard by the monkey-pod trees and think, "How beautiful".

Kids Gardens

Sometimes you will plant especially for kids. This is a wonderful way to introduce them to the Joys of Gardening. Plant a giant pumpkin with "Atlantic Giant" seeds. Plant sunflowers, plant taro, and tell the story of how taro is symbolic of the family. Plant a beanstalk. Things that grow fast are fun. Plant things they like to eat, such as snap peas, lettuces, radishes, and tomatoes. They will pick the peas right off the plant and eat them like candy. Even Buddy, the dog, nibbles a few cherry tomatoes now and then from the garden. Zinnias and cosmos are fun. Find ways to make it fun. Gardening should always be a joy, not a chore. Encourage creativity by allowing children to pick out their own seeds as you browse through the seed racks or catalogues. Stimulate them, and praise their efforts often. Make a garden design together on paper. This will teach children about imagining something in their minds, setting out to achieve that goal, and making it come true.

Evaluating the Garden

You will evaluate your garden continuously. There is always something to change. You will learn by observation, and trial and error, and from friends and other gardeners. There will be many successes! There will be plants to move, and changes to be made.

About Spontaneity

It's wonderful to be spontaneous and free, but certain things in life work best with a plan. Even a vague plan is fine, as the details can be worked out later. As in life, successful people write things down and accomplish each item one by one; and they make things happen. In gardening, you imagine in your dreams the setting you would like to achieve, then set out to create it!

Resources

<u>Rodale's Encyclopedia of Organic Gardening</u>

<u>Native Planters in Old Hawaii</u>
    By Handy Handy Pukui

<u>Garden Design Magazine</u>

<u>Organic Gardening Magazine</u>   Rodale Press

<u>Victoria Magazine</u>   (archives)

<u>Tropical Organic Gardening</u>   Richard Stevens

<u>Hawaiian Moon Calendar</u>

Web-Sites

- www.hawaiiorganicfarmers.org
- www.groworganic.com
- www.whiteflowerfarm.com

Do your own google.com searches for native plants, giant pumpkins, sunflowers, seeds, perennials, annuals, roses, and tools for the gardener.

Why Go Organic?

Chemical pesticides and fertilizers can increase production in the shortrun, but degenerate the land and cause soil erosion in the long run. Also, cancer-causing chemicals leak out and pollute the environment. Forty-five percent of the chemical residues stay on the fruits and vegetables. They can harm us.

Organic gardening conserves soil fertility. Organic farmers practice crop rotation, and recycle animal waste and plant residues (compost), to make the soil healthy, and to keep beneficial insects and pests in balance, thereby growing healthy crops.

(Hawaii Organic Farmers Association)

Weed Control

Pull weeds, mulch with heavy grass clippings, or use black plastic or shade cloth to prevent weeds from coming up. Try to stay on top of it before they get out of control! Don't be overwhelmed! Take small sections at a time and see it complete!

Remember

Gardening is good for the soul.

Gardening cultivates the body, mind, soul, and spirit.

Thank God for Gardening. Always ask for a blessing.

Gardens are like children. They need protection, loving care and nurturing, until established. Then they will do well on their own.

Gardening calms the spirit. Gardens heal emotionally.

Native Plantings restore the look of Old Hawaii.

Keep it wild if possible.

Be a seed saver.

Plant from cuttings.

Plants love it best in the earth.

© Copyright 2005 Marilyn Jansen

To order a copy of:
Amaryllis, Amaryllis How Does Your Garden Grow?
"Organically of Course!" and other books and products
by Marilyn Jansen, go to the web-site at:

www.amaryllisofhawaii.com

footnotes:

1. from the book Native Planters in Old Hawaii
by Handy, Handy, and Pukui
2. from the book The Man Who Planted Trees
by Jean Giono

All photography by Marilyn Jansen

A special thanks to my friend Marcia who influenced
me so much with her love of plants and nature, and
Catherine Lopes who loves to plant!
        printed in China